HORIZONS

Learning to Read

Level A
Textbook 2

Siegfried Engelmann

Owen Engelmann

Karen Lou Seitz Davis

SRA McGraw-Hill

Columbus, Ohio

A Division of The **McGraw·Hill** *Companies*

Illustration Credits

Anthony Accardo, Cindy Brodie, Daniel Clifford, Mark Corcoran, Doug Cushman, Susanne Demarco, Len Ebert, Frank Ferri, Kersti Frigell, Simon Galkin, Dara Goldman, Meryl Henderson, Dennis Hockerman, Gay Holland, Ann Iosa, Anne Kennedy, Pamela Levy, Loretta Lustig, Pat Morris, Margaret San Filippo, Pat Schories, Charles Shaw, Lauren Simeone.

SRA/McGraw-Hill

A Division of The McGraw-Hill Companies

Printed in the United States of America.

Send all inquiries to:
SRA/McGraw-Hill
8787 Orion Place
Columbus, OH 43240-4027

ISBN 0-02-674191-1

2 3 4 5 6 7 8 9 VHJ 01

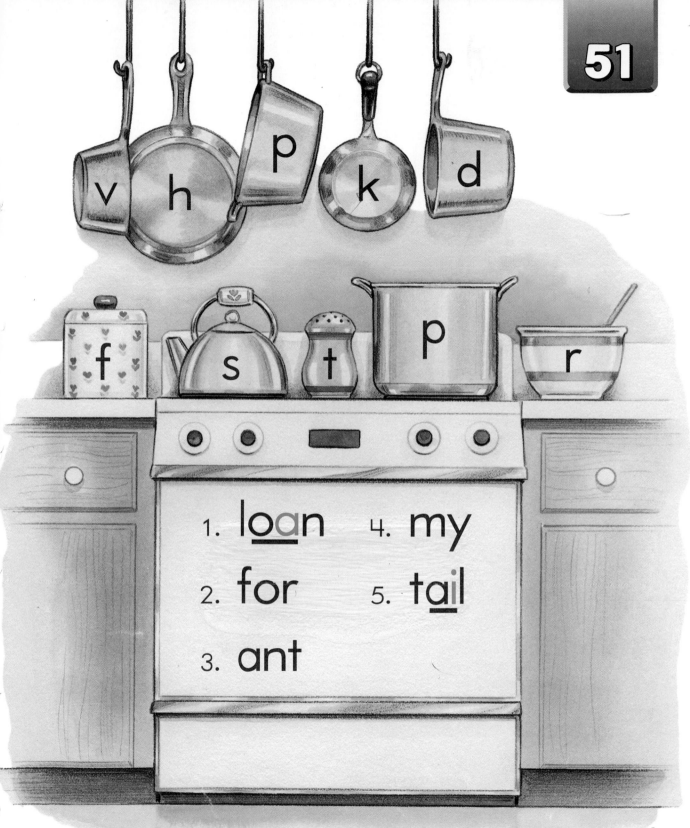

1. l<u>oa</u>n
2. for
3. ant
4. my
5. t<u>ai</u>l

1. <u>I</u> <u>see</u> <u>no</u> <u>ant</u>.
2. <u>I</u> <u>feel</u> <u>an</u> <u>ant</u>.

1

<u>I</u> <u>see</u> <u>no</u> <u>ant</u>.

k h v d

p a y p i

1. pal
2. l<u>ea</u>p
3. s<u>oa</u>p

1. fine
2. mile

1. s<u>ai</u>l

2. s<u>ea</u>l

3. n<u>ea</u>t

1. <u>See</u> <u>me</u> <u>sa</u>i<u>l</u>.
2. <u>I</u> <u>am</u> <u>a</u> <u>se</u>a<u>l</u>.

<u>See</u> <u>me</u> <u>sa</u>i<u>l</u>.

5

j k h j d

p
a i
y
e a
i
o a

1. fry
2. spy

1. ate
2. fine
3. safe

1. p<u>ai</u>l   2. pal

1. <u>I</u> feel <u>r</u>a<u>i</u>n.
2. <u>See</u> <u>me</u> <u>s</u>a<u>i</u>l.

j k v j h

p
i
f
y
t

1. pal
2. pan
3. so_p
4. fly

1. mile
2. note
3. late

See my pal eat.

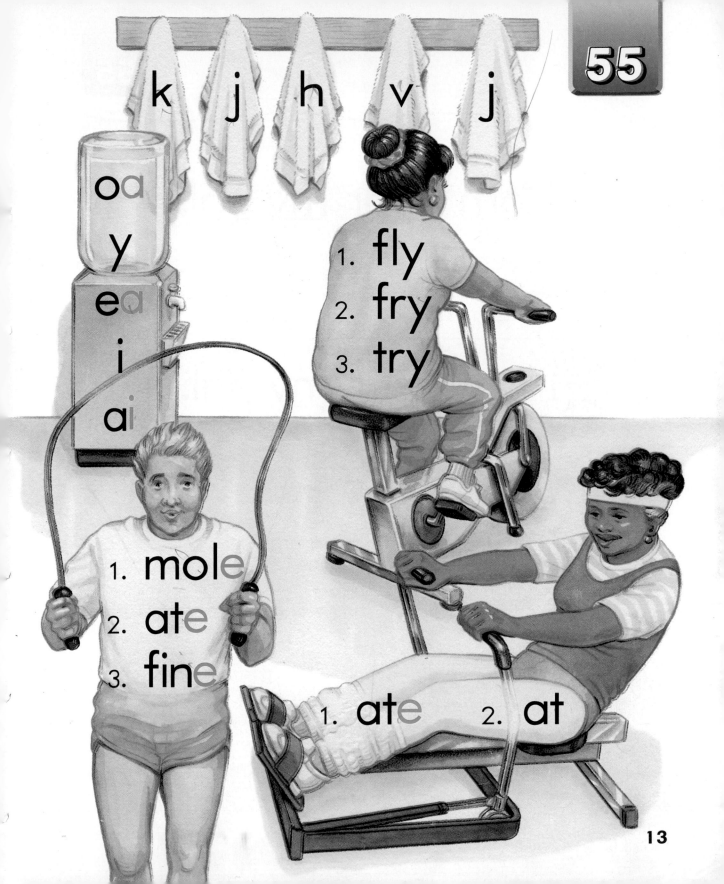

55

k j h v j

oa
y
e a
i
ai

1. fly
2. fry
3. try

1. mole
2. ate
3. fine

1. ate 2. at

13

I am n<u>ea</u>r my p<u>al</u>.

I am n<u>ea</u>r my pal.

j k c h c k

ai p oa t ea y

1. at
2. sat
3. rat

1. pan
2. tan
3. near
4. mail

1. sore 2. name
3. time

56

1. A ram ran at me.
2. I ran at a ram.

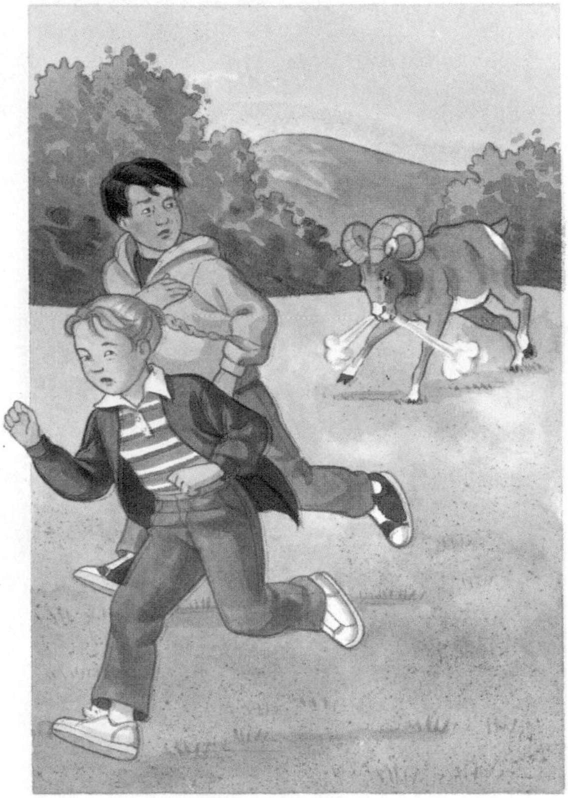

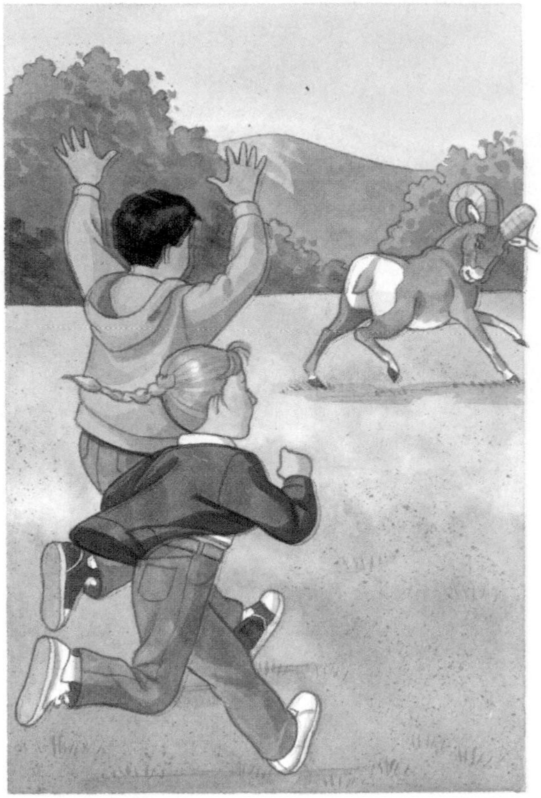

1. A ram ran at me.
2. I ran at a ram.

h c k j c d

th y p oa t th ai

1. <u>e</u>ar
2. an
3. or
4. feet

1. sat 2. safe
3. ate 4. at

1. I am <u>saf</u>e.

2. <u>My</u> <u>feet</u> <u>feel</u> <u>fin</u>e.

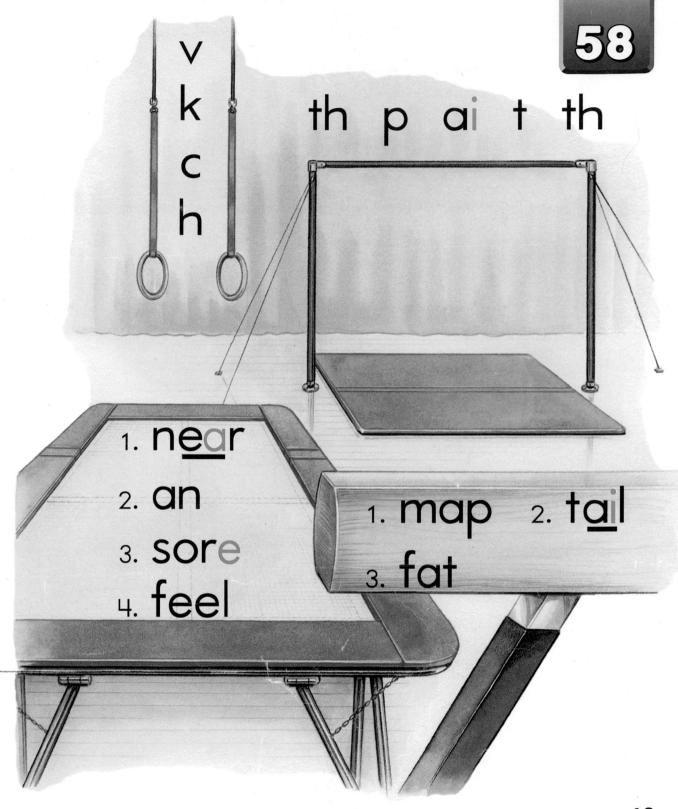

v
k
c
h

th p ai t th

1. ne**a**r
2. an
3. sor**e**
4. feel

1. map   2. t**ai**l
3. fat

1. I feel rain.
2. My feet feel fine.

☆ c ☆ w ☆ d ☆ w ☆ v

y i th ai p t th

1. fly
2. n<u>ea</u>r
3. feet
4. sat

1. pal
2. p<u>ai</u>l
3. pile

1. Sam
2. same
3. name
4. more

1. A fly sat near me.
2. My feet feel sore.

d c k v w j

ai t y p th oa

1. <u>th</u>at
2. <u>th</u>e
3. ma<u>th</u>

1. p<u>ai</u>l
2. pal
3. mol<u>e</u>
4. lat<u>e</u>

1. I am a fly.
2. I fly n<u>ea</u>r an <u>ea</u>r.

I am a fly.

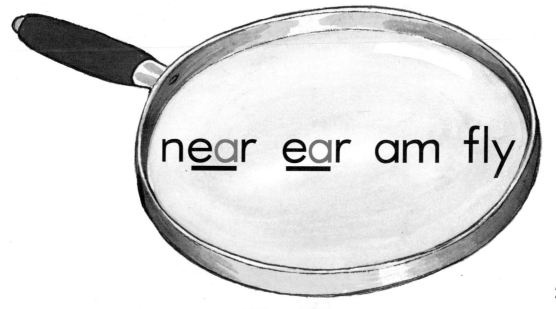

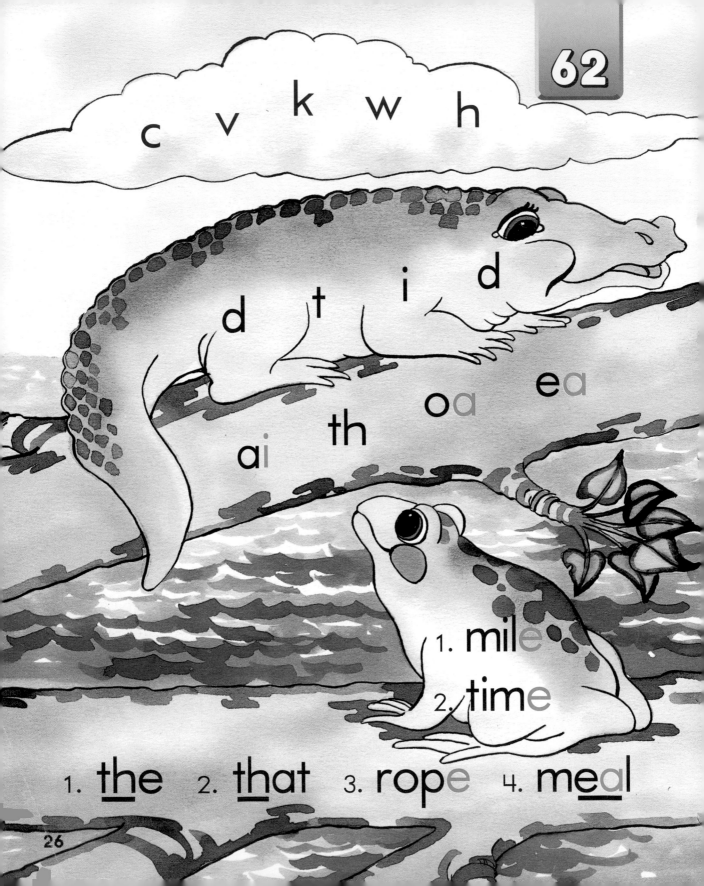

c v k w h

d t i d

ea

oa

ai th

1. mile
2. time

1. <u>th</u>e 2. <u>th</u>at 3. rop<u>e</u> 4. m<u>e</u>a<u>l</u>

1. I rope a ram.
2. See my pal fly.

I rope a ram.

w n g h g v

p d t d

1. ne<u>a</u>r
2. t<u>ea</u>r
3. m<u>ea</u>l

an

man

1. fine
2. pile
3. rope

1. I see a man fly.
2. I <u>ea</u>t a m<u>ea</u>l.

I see a man fly.

i a

time   mile

t p d n th y

1. r<u>ea</u>d
2. dad

1. name
2. map

<u>th</u>at

<u>p</u>a<u>th</u>

The ram ran at the man. So that man ran for a mile.

The ram ran at the man.

So <u>th</u>at man ran
for a mile.

1. pile
2. time

1. dad
2. r<u>o</u>ad
3. made

1. safe
2. rat
3. <u>pa</u><u>th</u>
4. name

34

A rat ran at a mole. So that mole ran near a pile.

A rat ran at a mole.

So <u>th</u>at mole ran
n<u>ea</u>r a pile.

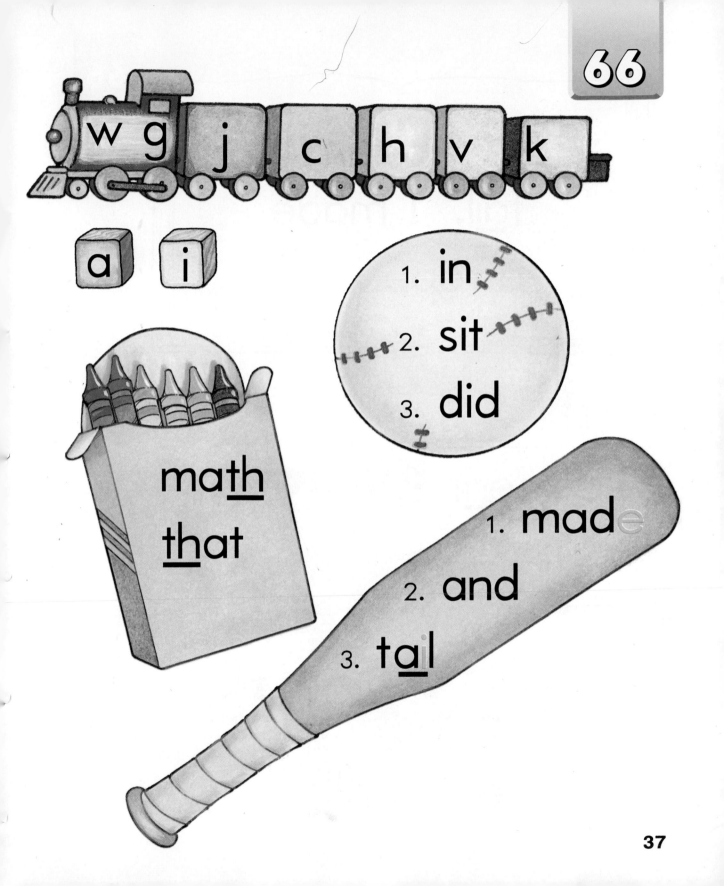

w g j c h v k

a i

1. in
2. sit
3. did

ma<u>th</u>
<u>th</u>at

1. mad<u>e</u>
2. and
3. t<u>ai</u>l

I sat near a tail. I made a rope.

I sat near a tail.

I made a rope.

v w c k j g

as
t<u>h</u>ose

i a

fin
did

f<u>o</u>am
s<u>oa</u>p

1. mad<u>e</u>
2. and

I see foam and a tail. I see no soap near me.

I see foam and a tail.

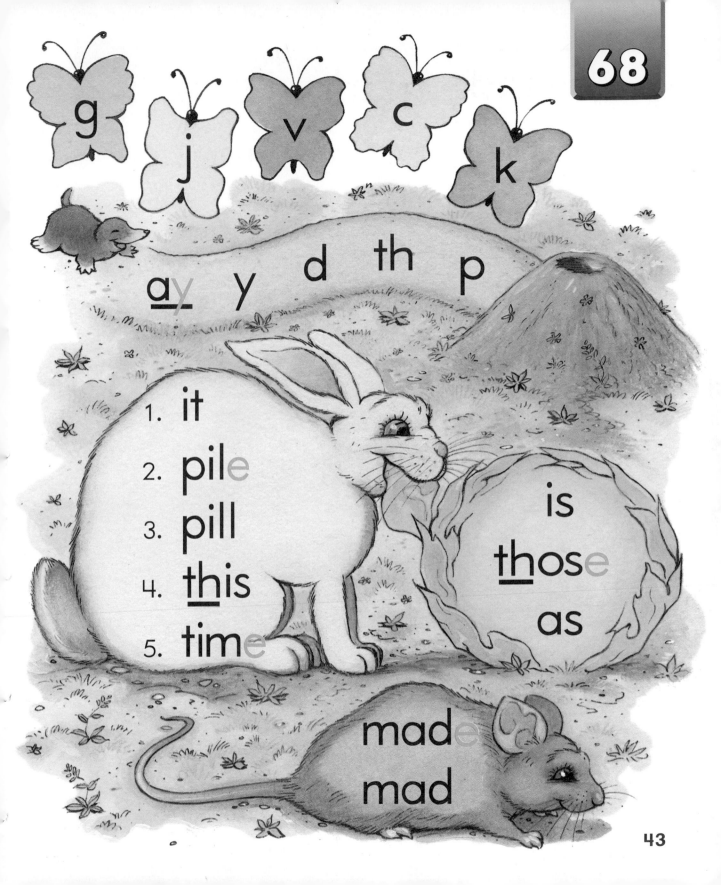

g j v c k

<u>a</u>y y d th p

1. it
2. pile
3. pill
4. <u>th</u>is
5. time

is
<u>th</u>ose
as

made
mad

43

A mole made a pile.
That pile made the
ram mad.

A mole made a pile.

<u>Th</u>at pile made <u>th</u>e
ram mad.

w   j   k   v   g   e

ay   th   d   t   y   p

1. is
2. as
3. <u>th</u>ese

1. try
2. fly
3. dry

1. time
2. <u>th</u>is
3. did

I see r<u>ai</u>n. So it is time for ma<u>th</u>.

It is time for ma<u>th</u>.

d

t

v

k

1. and
2. **th**ose
3. **th**ese
4. **th**at

1. s**ay**
2. d**ay**
3. m**ay**

I sit n<u>ea</u>r my pal. <u>Th</u>at pal is my dad.

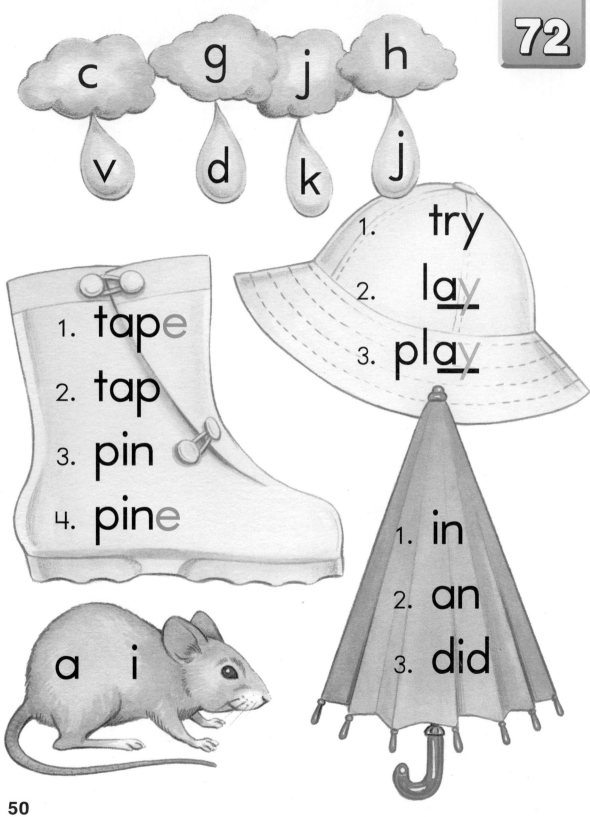

c
g
j
h

v
d
k
j

1. try
2. la__y__
3. pl__ay__

1. tape
2. tap
3. pin
4. pine

1. in
2. an
3. did

a   i

It is time for t̲h̲e mail. T̲h̲at ma̲i̲l is for me. My so̲a̲p is in t̲h̲at ma̲i̲l.

j | k

made
r**a**n

1. in
2. ant
3. sit
4. **th**at

1. s**a**~~y~~
2. pl**a**~~y~~

The rain made a ram sit. So that ram is mad.

The rain made me sit.

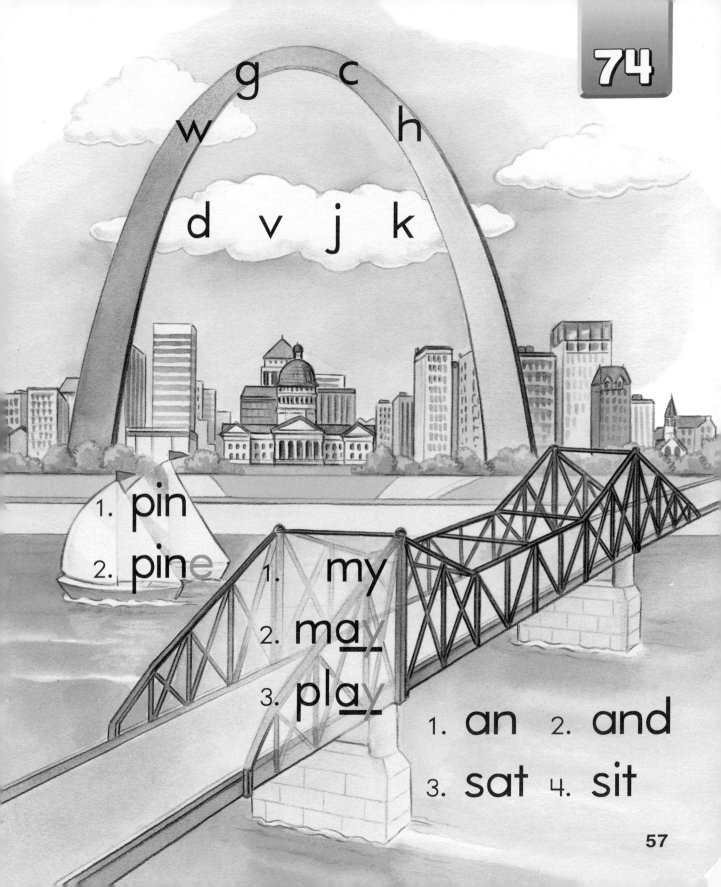

g c
w h

d v j k

1. pin
2. pine

1. my
2. may
3. play

1. an 2. and
3. sat 4. sit

My soap is in the mail. Rain made that soap foam. An ant is in the foam.

My soap is in the mail.

Rain made that soap foam.

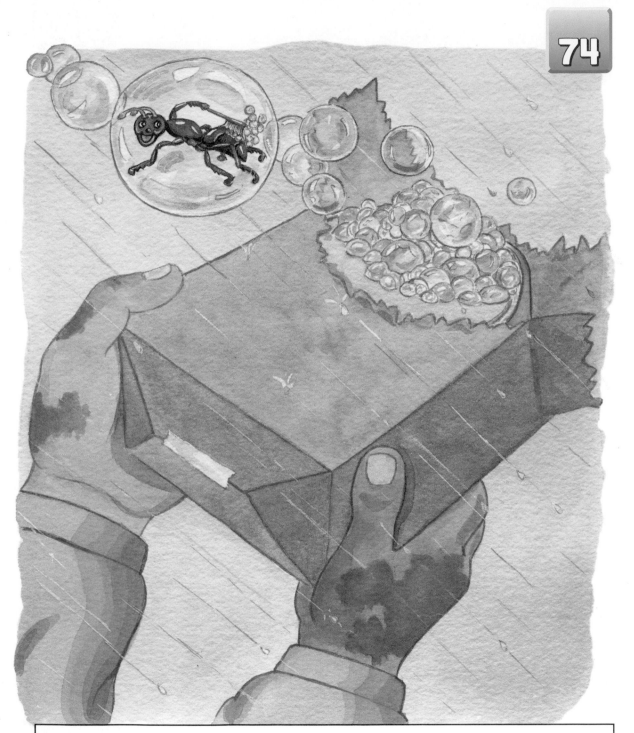

An ant is in <u>the</u> f<u>oa</u>m.

d   v   k   j

1. dive
2. make

1. rope
2. tail

1. tree
2. sleep
3. slip

Sam may eat a rope. That rope is no rope. It is a tail.

k v ck j c

than
and
ant

tree
trip
sleep

1. make
2. save
3. like
4. jail
5. van

A seal and a ram may play. Or the seal may sleep. And the ram may eat a sail.

A seal may sleep.

A ram m<u>a</u>y <u>e</u>at a s<u>ai</u>l.

v   c   k   j   d   ck

1. stove
2. dive
3. make
4. take

1. pill
2. pile
3. ride
4. sore

pin
need
tan

I see rain. My pal may play in the rain. Or my pal may eat.

I see rain.

My pal m<u>ay</u> pl<u>ay</u> in
th<u>e</u> r<u>ai</u>n.

Or my pal m<u>ay</u> <u>ea</u>t.

f c v k j ck

d

1. ja_l
2. stov
3. lik
4. tak

1. fine
2. fin
3. sore
4. ride

seed
need
tan

I like my pal. My pal may take me for a ride. That may make me sore.

I like my pal.

My pal m<u>ay</u> take me
for a ride.

That may make me sore.

c
v
k
j
ck
p

1. take
2. lake
3. joke
4. stove

1. old
2. drive
3. trip

pine
sleep
pa<u>th</u>

An ant is in a pine
tree. Is <u>th</u>at ant safe?
No.

An ant is in a pine tree.

Is <u>th</u>at ant safe?

th
ck
ay

v w n u

c j k

i a

1. cat
2. si**ck**
3. rak**e**
4. cold

pins
jokes
vans

1. old
2. sold
3. stor**e**
4. driv**e**

An ant is in a van. Is
a man in <u>th</u>at van?
No. See a mole drive.

An ant is in a van.

Is a man in <u>the</u> van?
No. See a mole drive.

v u y w

ck ay c j v

can
d**a**y
st**ay**

1. lakes
2. stores
3. trees

lip
slip

1. low 2. slow 3. you

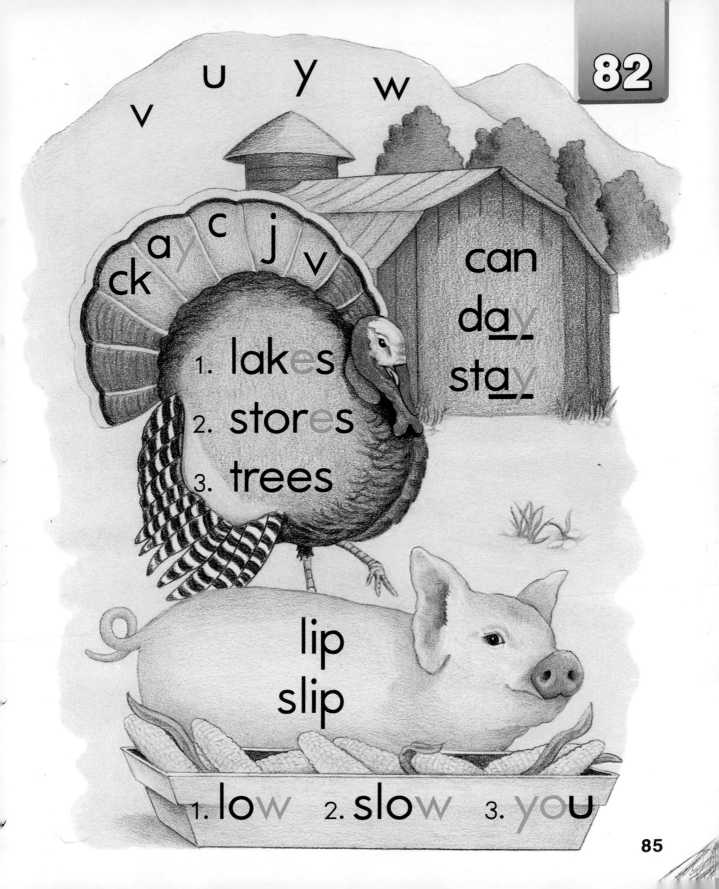

Is a rat near the lake? **82**
No. Is the rat in this
tree? No. Is that rat
in a store?

Is a rat near the lake?

Is <u>th</u>e rat in <u>th</u>is tree?

<u>Th</u>at rat is in a store.

h w n v

j ay ck v

1. lakes
2. rakes
3. jails
4. tails

1. pay
2. stay
3. cat
4. nap

1. old
2. told
3. cold

1. low
2. flow
3. you

Did the tan ram sleep?
No. Did that ram dive in
a lake? No. Did that
ram sit in the path? No.

Did the tan ram sleep?

Did <u>th</u>at ram dive in a lake?

Did <u>th</u>e tan ram sit in <u>th</u>e pa<u>th</u>?

1. know
2. no
3. slow
4. **<u>th</u>ose**

1. cats
2. rak**e**s
3. pals
4. naps

1. dim**e**
2. kit**e**
3. lid

A seal and 3 pals sat **84** near a lake. Those pals may play in the lake. Or those pals may take a nap.

A seal and 3 pals sat near a lake.

Those pals may play in
the lake.

Or those pals may take
a nap.

e k w h o

ai   ay

c   k

v   j

i   a

1. will
2. with
3. wide
4. we

1. these
2. those
3. path
4. trip

1. kicks
2. kites
3. cats
4. coats

A rake is in a path.
Cats play in that path.
Did the rake trip those
cats? No. These cats
can eat rakes.

A rake is in a path.

Cats pl**ay** in **th**at pa**th**.

85

Did the rake trip those cats? No. These cats can eat rakes.

r w g p c g

1. you
2. if
3. cats
4. store
5. tr<u>ai</u>n

1. sad
2. mad
3. made
4. make

1. win
2. will
3. wide

this with

A man is n<u>ea</u>r a lake.
A cat will trip that man.
Will that make the man
mad? You will see.

A man is n<u>ea</u>r a lake.

A cat will trip that man.

That made the man mad.

p d g c w

1. deep
2. keep
3. you
4. know

those
that

1. made
2. make
3. five
4. snow

1. said
2. trip
3. will

Cats ran in a store. A man made those cats sit. Did that make the cats mad? You will see.

Cats ran in a store.

A man made those cats
sit. Did that make the
cats mad?

1. needs
2. seeds
3. rakes
4. makes

w   g   c

1. said
2. over
3. snow
4. deep
5. we

1. seals
2. cold
3. five
4. trails
5. trains

A ram sat in the snow. That snow made the ram feel cold. The ram told five seals that the snow is cold. Did that make the seals mad? No. Those seals like cold snow.

A ram sat in the snow. That snow made the ram feel cold.

That snow is cold.

Did that make the seals mad? No.

p   g   w   c

to

do

1. needs
2. weeds
3. coats
4. trails

1. said
2. over
3. ask
4. snow
5. if
6. deep

It is a cold d<u>ay</u>. Snow is in the stove. A cat and a rat feel cold. Is an ant as cold as the stove? No. That ant is in five c<u>oa</u>ts.

It is a cold d<u>ay</u>. Snow is in the stove.

A cat and a rat feel cold. Is an ant as cold as the stove?

No. That ant is in five c<u>o</u>ats.

v c j g k w

1. to
2. do
3. over
4. said
5. ask

1. more
2. mail
3. make

go
pig

weeds
jokes
likes

117

A mole and a rat like to play. The rat likes to play in the weeds. The mole likes to play jokes.

A mole and a rat like to play.

The rat likes to play in the weeds.

The mole likes to play
jokes.

e h i o

k g c j v w

1. gave
2. games
3. dig

1. do
2. said
3. to
4. over

seeds
jokes
plays

1. more
2. make
3. take
4. sail

1. A mole said, "I play jokes."
2. A rat said, "Those jokes make me mad."
3. A ram said, "You play sick jokes."

I play jokes.

Those jokes make me mad.

You play sick jokes.

c h g j

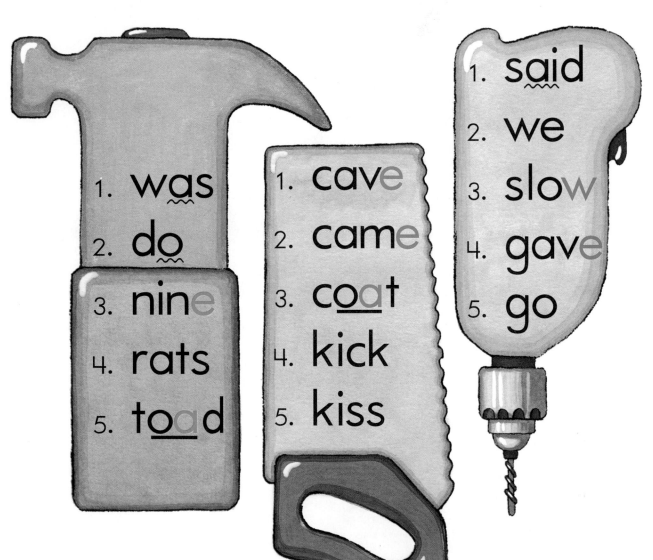

1. was
2. do
3. nine
4. rats
5. toad

1. cave
2. came
3. coat
4. kick
5. kiss

1. said
2. we
3. slow
4. gave
5. go

An ant said, "I like to sit." So that ant sat. Five rats said, "We like to sit." So those rats sat with the ant.

An ant said, "I like to sit." So that ant sat.

Five rats said, "We like to sit."

So those rats sat with
the ant.

y v u th h c g h

1. he
2. hill
3. hide

1. was
2. do
3. to
4. said

1. pig
2. toad
3. goat
4. came
5. mean

1. played
2. liked

A mean ant was near a toad. The toad said, "Do you like to play?"

The ant said, "No."

The toad said, "Do you like to sleep?"

The ant said, "No."

The toad said, "Do you like to eat?"

The ant said, "No."

The toad said, "I do."

So the toad did that.

i a u e

c j h w th g

1. had
2. hate
3. hill

1. wins
2. goats
3. waves

1. crow
2. green
3. read
4. need
5. note
6. fit

1. filled
2. sailed
3. lived

A goat ate and ate. The goat said, "I feel sick."

A mole told the goat, "You need to sit and read."

The mole gave the goat a note to read. Did the goat do that with the note? No. The goat ate it.

I feel sick.

u

h

n

c

g

1. green
2. grow
3. coat
4. note
5. fit

1. had
2. hide
3. hid
4. hold
5. home

1. smiled   2. lived   3. sailed
4. filled   5. kicked

A crow had a green coat. A goat said to the crow, "I like that coat."

The crow said, "No goat can fit in this coat."

The goat said, "May I try?"

A crow had a green coat.

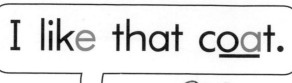

n h c

g v u

1. fit
2. green
3. crow
4. grow
5. gave

1. hike
2. had
3. has
4. home
5. hold

1. ask**ed**   2. kick**ed**   3. smil**ed**

4. kiss**ed**   5. lik**ed**

141

A crow had a green coat. A goat liked the coat. He said, "May I try that coat?"

So the crow gave the coat to the goat.

The goat said, "This coat will fit in me."

And the goat ate the coat.

May I try that coat?

The crow gave the c<u>oa</u>t to
the g<u>oa</u>t.

i c b a o

n u d w u h

1. us
2. run
3. up

1. the
2. him
3. his
4. hikes
5. hate

was
do
said

1. lived
2. asked
3. hiked

The crow was cold.

A ram was near. That ram had an old coat. The crow asked the ram, "Can I try that coat?"

The ram said, "This coat is for rams."

The crow said, "I can fit in that coat."

And he did.

The crow was cold. A ram was near. That ram had an old coat.

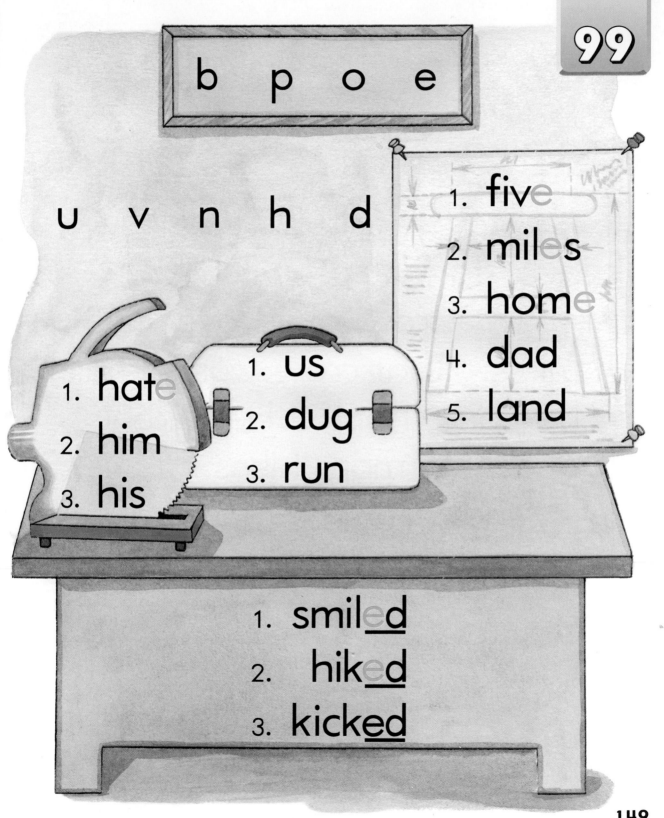

b p o e

u v n h d

1. hate
2. him
3. his

1. us
2. dug
3. run

1. five
2. miles
3. home
4. dad
5. land

1. smil**ed**
2. hik**ed**
3. kick**ed**

A crow told his dad, "I hate to fly, so I will hike."

The crow hiked over five miles. That crow was sad as he came home. He told his dad, "No more hikes for me."

That hike gave him sore feet.